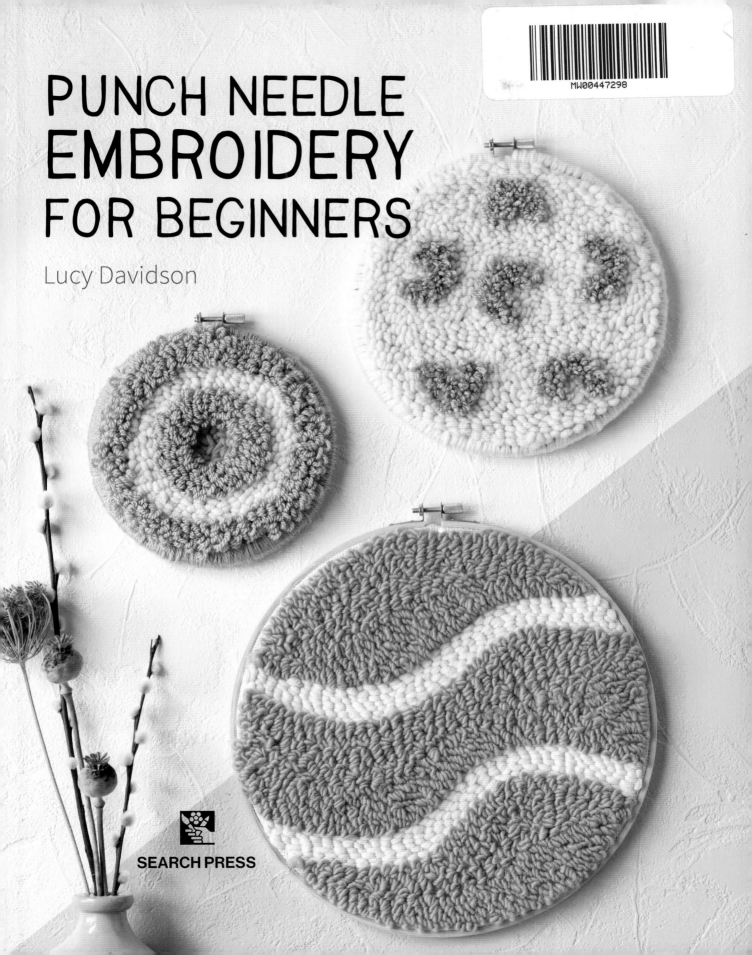

PUNCH NEEDLE
EMBROIDERY
FOR BEGINNERS

Lucy Davidson

SEARCH PRESS

CONTENTS

page 32

page 48

page 64

INTRODUCTION

I've always been obsessed with textiles and anything tactile, especially yarn. So much so, that I kept a ball of yarn for 10 years, which I had bought on a trip to New York for my twenty-first birthday, just waiting for the 'right project'. That project never came, but I just loved the texture and colour of this particular ball of yarn and couldn't bring myself to use it. Then, two years ago, it felt the right time to pass it on. I teach punch-needle and tapestry-weaving workshops, and at one workshop I decided that it would be best for this ball of yarn to be used by someone who was enjoying the experience with yarn in that class, and could add it to their own beautiful creation. It took a lot for me to let go of that ball of yarn.

Before I became obsessed with punch needle, I was constantly creating and drawing. I grew up in a very creative family, so even from an early age there was always something to make and it was always highly encouraged. As I got older I tried my hand at many crafts, which I documented on my blog, Peas and Needles; however, I didn't really stick with one until I came across weaving. It combined my love of yarn and the tangible side of craft. For years I created large, tactile, woven wall hangings, passing my skills on to others through teaching workshops. I then came across punch needle embroidery; I had absolutely no idea what it was, but as with my weaving I did a lot of research and taught myself how to needle punch. It quickly became my new favourite craft.

The projects in this book are for all skill levels. The first half, the techniques section, covers all the fundamental skills you'll need to create all the projects – including how to make your own wooden frame, which materials are best to use and to how to finish off your punch-needle artworks. So, even if you are a complete beginner, this book is still for you.

Writing this book has been such a joy, and I have loved every minute of it – from coming up with the designs for the projects to sitting down for many hours making them. I really hope you get as much enjoyment out of this book as I did writing it, and I do hope from reading this book you will have the confidence to create these delightful projects and your own pieces of fibre art, all whilst learning this beautiful craft.

MATERIALS & TOOLS
Punch needles

These are the main tools for the craft, and they come in all shapes and sizes. Some are adjustable and some are made for quick and easy loading. I will be mainly using the Amy Oxford Punch Needle in this book, which is for chunky (bulky) weight yarn. Don't worry if you don't have any chunky (bulky) yarn, you can thread multiple lengths of yarn in the same colour at the same time (more on this later).

1 UNIVERSAL LAVOR PUNCH NEEDLE SET

This set comes with three needle sizes and is perfect for punching with embroidery thread/floss – using all six strands – and DK (light worsted) weight yarns. You can adjust the loop height by twisting the screw, then moving the needle up or down. This needle is not suitable for extra chunky yarns. It is also quite small, so can be a little tricky to hold.

2 PLASTIC TWIST ADJUSTABLE PUNCH NEEDLES

There are two types of adjustable punch needles here – the Boye Punch Needle set [2a] and the Magic Embroidery Pen [2b]. Each set often comes with three needle sizes, so you can use three different weights of threads. It is ideal for designs that use embroidery thread/floss or lighter-weight yarns, for example DK (light worsted). Each needle size is adjustable too, so that you can change the height of your loops (see page 24 for more information). All adjustable needles need a threader (see **7**, opposite) to help you feed the thread/floss or yarn through the needle. I will show you how to do this on page 19.

3 OXFORD PUNCH NEEDLE, #10 REGULAR

These Oxford needles are designed by punch needle expert Amy Oxford. The Oxford Punch Needle is comfortable to hold, which is ideal for larger projects. These needles are also 'self-threading' (see page 18), so there is no need for a needle threader. The needle comes in various sizes; this size is the most common for punch needle as you can use it with chunkier yarns, or with doubled finer yarns. You can do this by threading two yarns through the tip of the needle at the same time. It can also be used with thin strips of fabric, which is more like traditional rug hooking.

4 OXFORD PUNCH NEEDLE, #14 FINE

Just like the #10 size, this needle is perfect for any larger projects. The wooden handle sits comfortably in your hand, as it is specially made to fit perfectly in your palm. The #14 is perfect for thinner yarns such as DK (light worsted) and tapestry yarn.

5 WOODEN ADJUSTABLE PUNCH NEEDLE (OR RUG PRODDER)

This needle is perfect for creating different textures and height in your work. The needle can be adjusted to make six different loop heights, from small to very large loops. The needle is also great for combining these stitches simply by twisting the metal needle inside the wooden handle, and moving it up or down and clicking into place. The longer the loops are the easier the needle is to use, as there is less chance of pulling the loops out of the fabric. Like the plastic adjustable needles, a needle threader (see **7**) is needed. Some models have different needle sizes, too, so that you can use different weights of threads.

6 PLASTIC SLIDE ADJUSTABLE PUNCH NEEDLE

This is very similar to the wooden adjustable punch needle, it is just made of plastic – unlike the others which are made for thinner yarns or embroidery thread/floss, this punch needle can be used for chunkier yarns.

7 NEEDLE THREADER

Most of the punch needles will need a threader [**7a**] to help feed your yarn though the needle. These often come with the actual punch needles, but if not you can just make your own using some thin wire [**7b**] – simply take a piece of wire a little longer than your needle, twist the end over to create a little 'eye' and thread it through your needle like you would with a purchased threader.

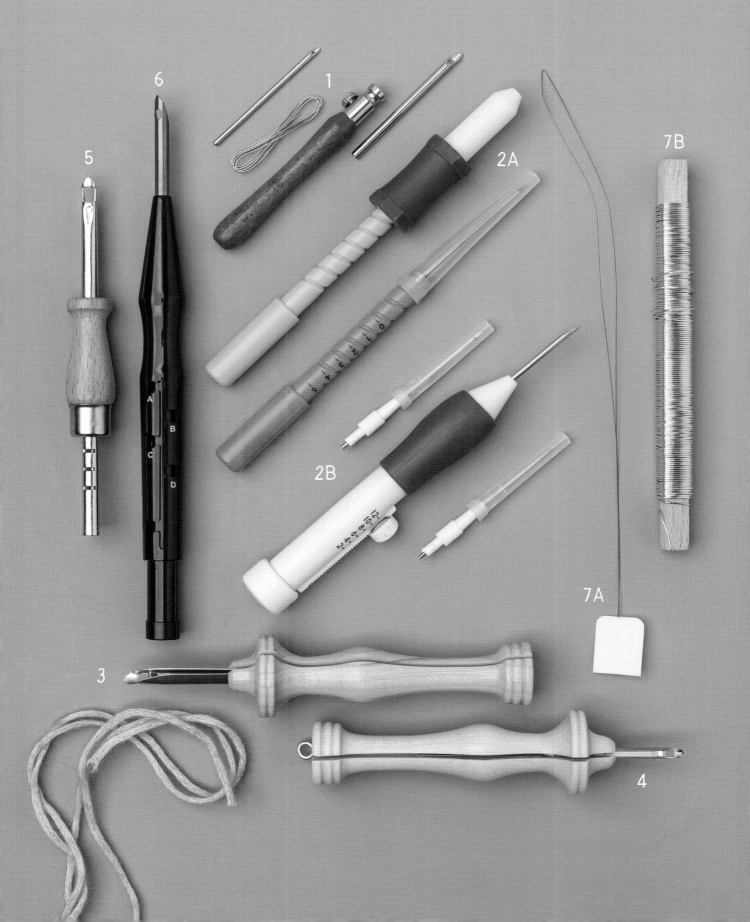

Essential tools

Most of these tools you will have lying around the house! This collection makes it easier for me to design and create my pieces; hopefully they will help you, too.

1 TAPE MEASURE OR RULER

I often use a fabric tape measure in my work; their flexibility makes them so useful. A ruler (not shown) is perfect for those straight lines and accurate measurements – handy for frame making (see page 15) and for transferring angular designs onto your fabric.

2 SMALL SCISSORS

Perfect for snipping those little stray pieces of yarn. Also, ideal for trimming loops to create little 'tufted' sections.

3 DRESSMAKING PINS

Pinning your fabrics together before you do any sewing on a sewing machine will help stop your fabric from slipping.

4 TASSEL MAKER

You could make tassels following the traditional method (winding the yarn around a strip of cardboard), however I like to use the adjustable tassel maker from Clover. Instructions on how to use this are on page 29.

5 DRAWING PINS/ THUMBTACKS

If you are using a wooden frame for holding your fabric (see page 16), use drawing pins/thumbtacks to temporarily secure the stretched fabric in place. These are more fiddly to use than a staple gun (see below), but are easier to remove.

6 STAPLE GUN

An alternative to drawing pins/ thumbtacks (see above), a staple gun is a quicker, slightly more secure way of holding your fabric once you've stretched it over the frame. The only con is the staples are trickier to remove afterwards!

7 FABRIC SCISSORS

Great for cutting the fabric for your project. Don't forget, only use these scissors for fabric and nothing else – especially not paper – as it will blunt them quickly.

8 POMPOM MAKER

Handy to have around if you want to embellish any of your projects with a pompom. Everyone loves a pompom!

9 HAND-SEWING NEEDLES

A pack of sewing needles will be extremely handy for hand sewing any last little bits together.

10 WOOL NEEDLE

You will need a wool needle for fastening off all the yarn ends that will be left on the punch needle work you create (see page 22).

11 MARKER PEN OR PENCIL

For drawing your designs straight onto the fabric. Try not to use any pens or markers that will bleed, or aren't waterproof; you don't want the ink to transfer onto your yarns.

12 GLUE

PVA glue, shown here, is useful for coating the back of your designs (see page 27). I also use other types of glue for adhering embellishments or non-punch-needled elements onto my design – either a hot-glue gun or strong craft glue.

13 PLIERS (NOT SHOWN)

Pliers are useful in case your adjustable punch needles become stuck or are too tight to unscrew by hand, and (conversely) tightening the screws effectively so the needles don't slip when you are working on your projects. I also use pliers to help attach hardware to my designs, such as magnetic snap fasteners.

14 SEWING MACHINE (NOT SHOWN)

For sewing together designs that combine your needle-punched design with regular sewing fabric.

Yarn & threads

You will notice in this book that I have stuck to a limited colour palette for the projects. However, you don't need to stick to these colours – experiment with your own materials and this way you will create a piece of work that is unique to you.

Wool-based yarn and threads are best for the beginner, as they are more durable and their texture means the loops are more likely to stay in the fabric.

You might have trouble if your yarn is too thin or too thick. The best way to test this is to see if your yarn slides in and out of your punch needle with too much ease, or without getting caught. If it's the correct thickness, the yarn will create the loops easily and won't fall out of your fabric (or get stuck).

Below are examples of some different materials you can use to create your punch needle loops. Using a variety of materials is a lovely way to create some texture in your work, and you can use up anything you have around the house. Remember: if you don't have any chunky (bulky) yarn, you can always use 4-ply (fingering) or DK (light worsted) weight yarn – but make sure to double or triple the yarn before threading it through. You can see below, in [D] and [E], where two and three yarns have been punched at the same time.

[A] Wool yarn

[B] Cotton

[C] Fabric strips

[D] Two yarns punched

[E] Three yarns punched

[F] Two different-coloured yarns

MATERIALS I HAVE USED

1   Rico Fashion Linen Swell Aran in 004 Salmon; 50g/120yd/110m.
    Alternative: aran (worsted) weight cotton-linen mix yarn in pink.

2   Glitter 4ply Metallic Yarn in 8F1 Coral; 200g/875yd/800m.
    Alternative: 4-ply (fingering) weight metallic yarn in pink.

3   Wendy Purity in 5165 Breeze; 50g/109yd/100m.
    Alternative: aran (worsted) weight cotton-merino wool mix chainette yarn in a peach colour.

4   Knitcraft Everyday DK in Mint Green; 50g/150yd/137m.
    Alternative: DK (light worsted) weight acrylic yarn in pale green.

5   DMC Natura Just Cotton Medium in 09; 50g/82yd/75m.
    Alternative: DK (light worsted) weight cotton yarn in yellow.

6   West Yorkshire Spinners Re:Treat in Mellow; 100g/153yd/140m.
    Alternative: chunky (bulky) weight 100% wool roving yarn in gold.

7   Women's Institute Soft and Chunky in Cream; 100g/120yd/110m.
    Alternative: chunky (bulky) weight acrylic-merino wool mix yarn in cream.

8   Women's Institute Home Cotton Aran in Pewter; 100g/175yd/160m.
    Alternative: aran (worsted) weight cotton-polyester mix yarn in pale grey.

9   DMC Natura Just Cotton Medium in 87; 50g/82yd/75m.
    Alternative: DK (light worsted) weight cotton yarn in jade green.

10 Cotton thread – It's ideal to have a cotton thread that matches the colour of the fabric or edge of the punched cloth. Use this thread with your sewing machine when sewing your projects together.

NOT SHOWN –

- Lily Sugar 'n Cream in Jute; 50g/120yd/109m.
  Alternative: aran (worsted) weight 100% cotton yarn in taupe.

- Anchor Creativa Fino 4ply in Fawn; 50g/136yd/125m.
  Alternative: 4-ply (fingering) weight 100% cotton yarn in brown.

TIP

As the needle is quite thick, your punch needle will leave a decent-sized hole in the fabric. For this reason, it's important that the yarn is thick enough to stay securely in the fabric. If the yarn that you like isn't quite thick enough, simply twist two or three yarns together, and punch them into the fabric in exactly the same way as you would with a single strand of yarn.

Fabrics

Your choice of fabric for your punch needle work is really important, as the weave needs to be nice and strong. Each one of these fabrics is slightly different, but you will soon find out which one you prefer. For a beginner, I would highly recommend starting with monk's cloth.

1 LINEN

Linen is suitable for both finer and chunkier yarns and threads/floss. Your needle will simply glide in and out of the holes, and linen works well especially with the adjustable punch needle and the Oxford Punch Needle. It is a great alternative if you are allergic to hessian.

2 COTTON MONK'S CLOTH

Monk's cloth is the ideal cloth for punch needling. It is made from a strong and durable cotton, and sits nice and taut in the frame. It is also made with a double thread on both the warp and weft, allowing you to remove stitches easily without distorting the fabric too much. The cloth comes with white lines every 5cm (2in) which helps to guide you when stretching the fabric. Ideally, look for fabric with 13 holes per inch. All the projects in this book are made with monk's cloth.

3 HESSIAN/BURLAP/JUTE

Hessian is the cheapest option and is easier to come by than other punch needle fabrics. When you are choosing your hessian, make sure you choose a good quality one with a close weave. It also comes in a variety of colours. It is not as soft as the other two fabrics, and is more suitable for DK (light worsted) and chunky (bulky) weight yarns.

Frames

It's extremely important that your fabric stays nice and tight whilst you are working on your piece, as it helps to keep your loops in place. To achieve this you will need a nice sturdy frame to stretch your fabric over. Below are a few different frames you can use for this.

1 WOODEN FRAME

These are perfect for larger projects, as wooden frames are very sturdy. You can make a frame to any size you need – see page 15 for instructions on how to do this. Then, lay your fabric over the top of the frame and either pin the fabric with drawing pins/thumbtacks or secure it with staples and a staple gun. Pin or staple small sections at a time, so that you can adjust the tension as you go.

2 TAPESTRY CLIP FRAME

This is an easy secure frame that is ideal for most sizes of punch-needled work. Simply place your piece of fabric over the frame and use the clips to secure the fabric. Twist the clips to tighten the fabric and you will be ready to punch in no time.

3 EMBROIDERY HOOPS

These are extremely easy to come by and are suitable for smaller projects. You can get these in all sizes, and I recommend investing in the non-slip variety. Place your fabric over the inner circle, place the outer circle over the top and push down. Stretch the fabric as you tighten the screw to secure the tension.

4 OLD PICTURE FRAME (NOT SHOWN)

There is no need to make your own wooden frame if you have any old wooden picture frames lying around! Or you could pick one up from your local charity shop/thrift store. Take the glass and backing out of the frame and then stretch your fabric in the same way as you would with a wooden frame.

5 STRETCHER BARS (NOT SHOWN)

These are easy to find in art shops as they are often bought by artists to make a DIY canvas. They can be purchased in pairs or as a pack of four. The bars have slots and wedges at each mitred end, so all you need to do is push the bars together and you'll have a secure frame. These are quite handy if you would like a big frame but are limited on storage space! One thing to remember is that these bars often have a bevelled 'picture' side, so you will need to stretch your fabric over this to pin or staple on the flatter back of the frame.

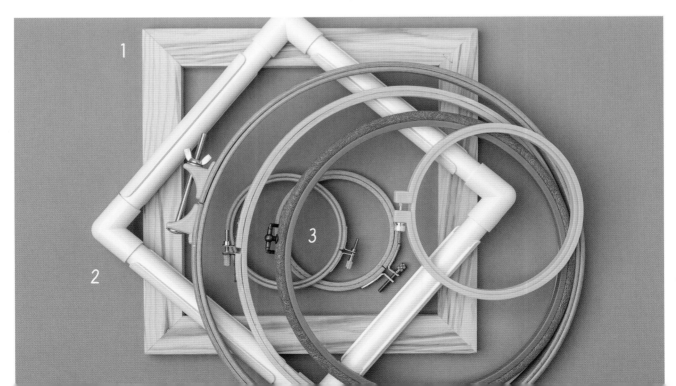

TECHNIQUES

Framing your fabric

Framing your fabric stretches it taut, allowing you to punch the fabric successfully and to free up your hands for punching correctly. If the fabric is too slack, it will make it difficult to punch the fabric and the loops will fall out.

If your design is small, you should be able to fit it within the frame or hoop; however, if your design is larger, such as the Rug on page 68, I would recommend using a larger wooden frame (see how to make your own, opposite) so that you can avoid re-framing your fabric.

Instructions for stretching your fabric in a wooden frame and an embroidery hoop are described below and on the next page. Purchased tapestry and embroidery clip frames often include detailed instructions on how to place fabric inside them, so I have not described them here.

PREPARING A HOOP

Embroidery hoops are ideal for smaller punch needle designs. I tend to use a 25cm (10in) diameter embroidery hoop. Quilting hoops are ideal if you would like an even larger size – I have seen some which have a diameter as large as 58cm (23in).

Always ensure that you have at least 5–7.5cm (2–3in) extra fabric around your design if you are using a hoop.

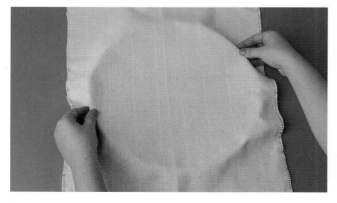

1 Detach the two rings that make up the embroidery hoop, then lay the smaller, inner hoop on a flat surface in front of you. Centre your fabric over the top.

2 Place the outer ring over the top of your fabric. Tighten the screw a little. Once the fabric is firmly in between the hoops, turn the hoop over so the back of the fabric is visible. Starting from the area near the screw, gently pull the fabric towards you and work your way around the hoop. Tighten the screw to secure your fabric.

MAKING YOUR OWN WOODEN FRAME

To do this, you will need one or two long, square-edged planks of wood (their lengths depend on how big you want your frame to be), a pencil, a tape measure, a hand saw (a cross-cut or string saw is fine) or electrical saw (such as a jigsaw), a protractor and a staple gun. If you have one, a mitre cutter would be very handy!

1 Measure, mark and cut four lengths from your planks of wood – the wood I have cut is roughly 40cm (15¾in) long, 3.5cm (1⅜in) wide and 1.8cm (about ¾in) thick.

Lay the pieces in the shape of a square or rectangle on a flat surface in front of you. With a pencil and protractor, mark angles at each end to mitre the wood accurately – remember, one end of the wood should slope 45 degrees to the right, the other end should slope 45 degrees to the left. This is so that the rightwards end can butt against the leftwards end.

When you are happy with the angles, mitre the edges of each wood piece with a saw or mitre cutter. Once all four pieces are mitred, butt the ends together.

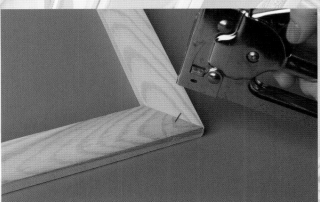

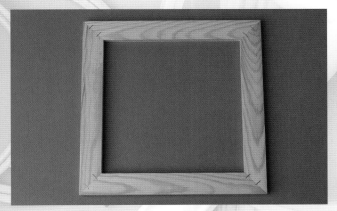

2 Staple the corners with the staple gun from the outer corners, as shown.

3 Repeat once more towards the inside of the frame, to secure each corner of the frame.

TIP

Choose a wood that is relatively soft, such as pine or spruce – these are not only easier to cut, but are easier to staple and pin your fabric to later!

I also recommend choosing planks of wood that are not too wide or too thick – no more than 4.5cm (2in) wide or 2.5cm (1in) deep. If the frame is too wide or thick, you will need more fabric to stretch around the frame, meaning more fabric wastage.

TIP

If cutting your own wooden frame sounds nerve-wracking, you can use an old picture frame – ideally, one made from softwood and without any coat or finish.

PREPARING A FRAME

Frames are perfect for angular designs and – if you have made one from scratch – they can be tailored to a particular size, too.

To account for the width of the frame, I advise marking the outline of your design to centre it accurately within the middle of the frame, and to help you see if there is too much fabric distortion when you are stretching the fabric over the edges. Furthermore, you will need to ensure there is at least 15–20cm (6–8in) of extra fabric around your design, so that you can stretch it happily around the frame.

I tend to use drawing pins/thumbtacks for stretching my fabric over a frame; however, if you prefer, you could use a staple gun and staples.

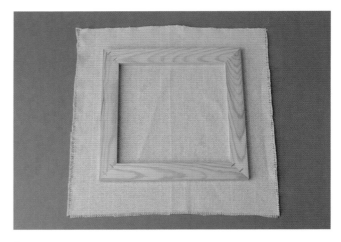

1 Lay your fabric on a flat, hard surface, then centre the frame over the top.

2 On one side, fold over the edge of the fabric by 6mm (¼in), then by 6mm (¼in) once more to double hem – this stops the fabric from fraying. Fold it over the side of the frame you are working on, and hold it in place with your fingers.

3 Place a drawing pin/thumbtack through the fabric and into the wood, at the centre of the frame. With the centre point secure, add pins at either side. Repeat, working your way outwards. Depending on the length of the wood, you can use just a few pins/thumbtacks, or several.

4 Repeat steps 2 and 3 until all the straight edges are folded over and secure. Firmly pull the fabric each time, to ensure the fabric is stretched relatively tightly around the frame.

5 To secure a corner, pinch the overlapping fabric together at one corner and fold it to one side. Trim away the excess fabric by about 2.5cm (1in).

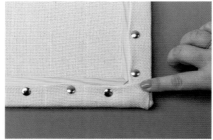

6 Fold the fabric in on itself, then once more to hide the cut edge and create a straight edge, as shown. Pin the edge in place with drawing pins/thumbtacks to secure.

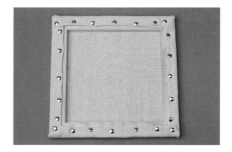

7 Repeat steps 5 and 6 three more times to finish framing your fabric.

Transferring patterns to fabric

Once you have created your design, or chosen the outline from the template sheet included in this book, you will need to transfer it onto your fabric, ready for you to punch needle. Follow the steps below for quick and easy ways on how to do this.

METHOD 1

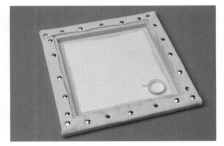

1 Trace, print off or photocopy the design you require onto a blank piece of paper.

2 With your fabric stretched over your frame (see page 14 or the opposite page for help with this), place the paper under the fabric, with the design facing the fabric. Use sticky tape to hold the paper in place.

3 Take your marker pen and trace the design straight onto your fabric – you may need to place a source of light behind your frame, such as a light box or day-lit window, to help you see the design from the back. Don't worry if you make a mistake, the punch needle stitches will hide all the marks.

METHOD 2

With your marker pen and chosen design to hand, draw freehand straight onto the stretched fabric. This method results in a design with a more unique, hand-made feel.

TIP

Why not combine a few of the elements from a couple of different projects in this book? This, way your piece will be one of a kind.

Punch needle 101

In this section, you will discover the key techniques to get you started on your punch needle journey.

I will be creating a needle-punched sampler throughout, just to show you how versatile, tactile and easy punch needling can be! If you wish, you could create a similar sampler yourself to build your confidence, and I have included the motifs for it on Template Sheet A.

The punch needle technique works by forming continuous loops with the yarn that are then secured in cloth. The tension of the yarn and cloth keeps your project from unravelling. This is why it's so important to have the correct fabric and yarn, as it will make the whole process so much easier. Just follow the key techniques below – I promise the stitches won't fall out!

HOW TO THREAD YOUR NEEDLE

The Oxford Punch Needle (see needles **3** and **4** on page 6) is non-adjustable and has an open shaft, so does not need a needle threader to help pull the yarn through the channel running along its length.

HOW TO THREAD AN OXFORD PUNCH NEEDLE

1 With the open-channel facing up, thread the yarn down through the eye at the tip of the needle, until there is a 10cm (4in) length of yarn hanging from the eye.

2 Holding on to the tail of yarn with one hand, use the other hand to slip the ball end of the yarn down and through the slot in the wooden handle.

3 Still holding on to the tail, pull the yarn at the end of the needle to secure it in the channel. Gently tug the yarn back and forth to make sure it is threaded correctly and there is no tension.

HOW TO THREAD AN ADJUSTABLE PUNCH NEEDLE

Adjustable needles will need a needle threader to pull the yarn through the centre, as their channels are enclosed. This technique applies to almost all types of adjustable punch needles.

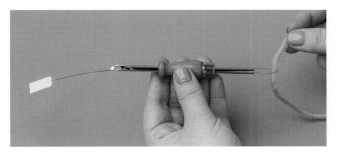

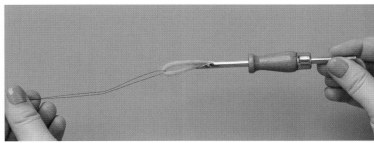

1 Take the yarn threader and insert it into the punch needle from the tip – the 'paper' end should be near the eye of the needle. Push the threader through the needle shaft completely until the metal looped end pokes out the other side. Insert the yarn into the metal loop.

2 Pull the threader back out of the needle; the yarn will follow and the yarn tail will pop out. Remove the yarn threader.

3 Poke the yarn tail back through the eye at the tip of the needle, as shown. If you wish, use the threader once again to do this: simply insert the threader through the eye of the needle from the flat-edged side of the needle tip. Thread the yarn and pull through.

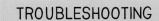

TROUBLESHOOTING

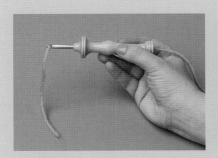

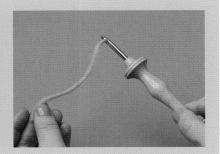

- Always leave a 10cm (4in) yarn tail hanging from the tip.

- The yarn tail must come out of this side of the needle (the flat edge), or else the loops won't form properly in the fabric.

- Make sure the ball end of the yarn isn't too taut; if there is too much tension, it will pull the loops out of the fabric. This is not good, as punching the fabric leaves holes, and it is difficult to punch back into the same hole in some fabrics. The picture, above, shows the correct tension – see how loose it is?

CREATING LOOP STITCHES

Typically, you will be punching the stretched side of the fabric to create the main design.

Like traditional rug hooking, this means you will be making slightly flatter stitches on the 'front' – the side from which you are punching – to create the main, fuller loop stitches on the 'back'.

In other words, the back of your design will be the front of your work when you finish!

All punch needles use the same technique.

1 Take the threaded needle and place the tip of the needle onto the fabric – the flat edge of the needle should be facing down (if you are using an Oxford Punch Needle, handily you can tell if the needle is the right way as the open slot along the length of the handle will be facing up).

2 Punch the needle right down into the fabric until the wooden handle meets the fabric. Take care that the 10cm (4in) tail of yarn is still in place.

MY LOOPS AREN'T FORMING. WHAT'S WRONG?

• Make sure your needle opening is facing the way you are punching, and that you are punching all the way down into the fabric.

• Check that the yarn is not getting caught on anything; there should be no tension on the yarn. For help with tension, see the Troubleshooting box on page 19.

• Your fabric might be loose. It's a good idea to keep checking the tension as you punch, and pull the fabric taut if you notice it is a little slack.

• Your yarn might be too thick. If you have trouble feeding it through your needle, maybe try a thinner yarn.

• Don't forget – if you are using monk's cloth, which I recommend for beginner punch needle artists, you can easily undo the entire row and redo it without damaging your fabric too much.

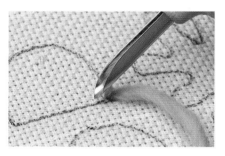

3 Bring the needle back out of the fabric, just enough to skim the top of the fabric. Don't bring it too high as this will create unwanted loops on this side. Skim the needle across the fabric by about 5mm (¼in), as shown, then punch down again.

4 Repeat steps 2 and 3 – they'll look like small running stitches. If you are right-handed, punch from right to left; if you are left-handed, punch from left to right.

WHAT SHOULD MY STITCHES LOOK LIKE?

• [**1**] just right, [**2**] stitches are a bit too loose, [**3**] stitches are a bit too tight.

• Use the weave of the fabric to help you count the distance between each stitch.

• The Oxford Punch Needle often comes with a 'stitch gauge', which can help you see how many stitches you should have in a 6cm (2½in) square.

FILLING IN A SHAPE

Once you have mastered the basic loop stitch, you can start working on larger projects that require bigger shapes that need filling in. There are two ways of doing this, which I will show on the right.

Always punch the outline or perimeter of a shape first before filling in the rest of the shape. This is especially important when you are trimming the beginning and finishing tails of yarn at the end of a project: once the fabric is completely filled with stitches, the loops are quite compacted together, making the whole design secure enough for any tails of yarn to be trimmed flush without the piece coming apart.

To fill in the background around all your shapes, follow exactly the same process! Punch the outline of the background area first then work your way in. If there are any gaps as you work, simply fill these in at the end.

1 Punch around the outline of the shape first.

2 Once you have completed the outline, begin a new row within the outline you've just made. Continue all the way around the shape, to create an inner outline.

3 Repeat this process, working smaller and smaller outlines within the shape, until you have filled in the whole motif.

4 Alternatively, work left to right in rows, to create a more linear stitch pattern in your shape.

CHANGING COLOURS

1 Work the shape intended in the first colour. When you wish to change to another colour, gently pull the needle away from your work (at the 'front'), carefully holding the end of the yarn closest to the work to prevent the stitch from being pulled out.

2 Cut the yarn, taking care to leave a 10cm (4in) tail of yarn.

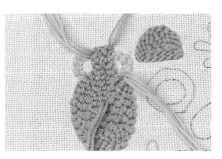

3 Rethread your needle then start to punch with your new colour.

FASTENING OFF

Below is the method I use for fastening off all yarn tails. You should do this once the yarn tail is surrounded by stitches, as this helps to secure the cut yarn. If the yarn tail – especially the beginning tail at the edge of a motif – is not yet surrounded by stitches, hold off cutting this until it is. Alternatively, if you're nervous, fasten off all tails once the whole design is in place.

1 As done for the Changing Colours technique on the previous page, once you have come to the end of your design, gently pull the punch needle away from the fabric at the 'front', making sure to catch the yarn with the other hand.
Note that for this particular shape, to achieve the thickness I wanted, I doubled the yarn so there are two strands of yarn.

2 Leaving a 10cm (4in) length on the 'front' of you work, cut the yarn. Thread the yarn tail or tails onto your wool needle.

3 Poke your needle through the centre of one of the stitches...

4 ... and pull your needle out the other side (the 'back' of your work).

5 The yarn tail should now be anchored, as it is 'squished' inside the stitch. Cut off the excess yarn flush against the stitching on the 'back' of your design.

Adding texture

One of the things I love to do with my work is create texture – I really love my work to be tactile. Here are a few simple techniques that can help you add some texture to your piece, giving it a unique and interesting finish.

CREATING EMBROIDERY STITCHES

You have learnt already that the punching you do on the 'front' creates the loop stitches on the 'back'. Well, if you like the look of the flatter stitches on the 'front' – which I like to call embroidery stitches – you can simply flip your frame or hoop over and work these on the 'back'! The contrast between loop and embroidery stitches creates a nice textural effect, and is very easy to achieve.

Below, I am combining both loop and embroidery stitches in a motif, to show the difference between the two stitches but also to make an interesting, varied surface for my punch needle design.

1 To begin my combined motif, I worked the outline of my design with the standard loop stitch. However, you could go straight into step 2!

2 Flip your frame over, so the 'back' of the work is facing you. Remember, this will be the side on display, once you finish your work.

3 As with regular loop stitching, start to punch on the 'back' of your work, from the outside of the shape inwards. Your flat 'front' stitches (the embroidery stitches) are now on the opposite side! You will see that it creates a lovely texture and can draw the eye to certain sections of your work.

4 The finished motif! Why not use this technique to highlight particular sections of your work, and create a lovely tactile piece?

The 'front' side of the work. See how the white yarn is creating loop stitches on this side? Why not try it this way round on your own design?

CREATING DIFFERENT LOOP HEIGHTS

To create different loop heights I recommend using an adjustable punch needle, as you can easily create consistent, various loop heights on it by simply changing the settings.

Unfortunately, you cannot adjust the loop height on the Amy Oxford Punch Needle. However, on the 'back' of your work, you could hold onto the loop and pull on it to make it larger. The only trouble with this is you are less likely to make consistent loops across your work.

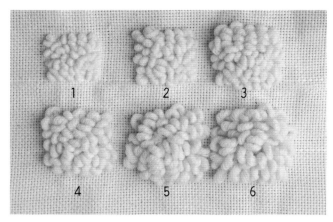

The variation in height you can achieve when you use an adjustable punch needle.
The loops range from small [1] to large [6].

1 Depending on your chosen adjustable needle, you will have a number of notches on the shaft that allow you to change the height of your loops. I would advise checking the manual of your particular type before beginning. The wooden adjustable punch needle I am using has six settings, indicated by the notches in the metal shaft at the back of the needle.

Currently, the needle is set at the first notch, so the yarn is closest to the eye of the needle. This creates the smallest loop size, which is approximately 2cm (¾in) high.

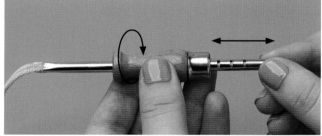

2 To adjust, simply twist the handle of the needle then push or pull the metal shaft until you feel the spring inside the handle snap into your chosen notch.

Here, I have twisted my needle to the third notch, which creates medium-sized loops. See how the needle has increased in length? I recommend this setting to start with, when you first begin to play with loop heights.

3 To create long loops (especially great for tufting) adjust your needle to the last setting, which creates loops about 6cm (2½in) high. You can see the needle is now very long.

4 To create the loops, simply punch the fabric from the 'front' as usual, following the Creating Loop Stitches technique on page 20. You can see on the 'back' how tall the loops are!

CREATING TUFTS

Add pompom-like tufts to your embroidery for a piece with lots of texture!
You will need an adjustable punch needle for this technique.

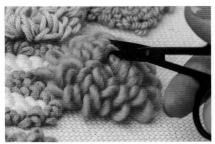

1 Set your adjustable punch needle to the largest loop height. Punch the stitches into the 'front' of your piece.

2 When you turn your work over, you will notice that you have a small bunch of long loops. Using a pair of small, sharp scissors, start to trim the loops.

3 Once you have trimmed all the loops you will be left with a small tuft! This creates a lovely tufted section that will add character to your piece.

Tufted shapes in the medium hoop of the Hoop Art Trio (see page 36).

BUILDING STITCHES

There are various ways you can build stitches. This is exactly how it sounds – piling stitches on top of each other to create impressive, 3D motifs. Below are two methods I like to use the most. I haven't used them in the projects for this book but, like the yarn colours, feel free to incorporate these into your own interpretations wherever you'd like!

EXAGGERATED STITCHES

I recommend using this method for smaller motifs, as it involves taking the yarn a greater distance across the fabric than regular punching. You can create some lovely looking punch needle flowers this way.

1 Flip your work over so that the 'back' of the piece is facing you.
2 Punch from one edge of the drawn outline. However, instead of working around the shape, swing backwards so your needle is next to your first stitch.
3 Punch the second stitch from the same edge again, this time making the length of the stitch a little longer and bringing the yarn slightly over the first stitch.
4 Repeat across the whole shape, gradually increasing the length of your stitches. Make sure, as your stitches get longer, to hold each loop of yarn under the work with your other hand as you punch. This secures the loop you're working on before beginning the next one.

COUCHED STITCHING

If you're familiar with regular embroidery, this will be a fun technique to recreate on a larger scale!

1 Wind a long length of yarn into a small hank (not too chunky, mind you!) and lay it over your chosen area.
2 Holding it in place with your fingers, simply punch over the hank – using an adjustable needle set to the largest loop size will help with this.

I have only punched the middle section to hold it in place; however, if you wish, you could punch over the whole hank to create a chunky 3D shape.

Finishing off

When you have completed your piece you will want to finish it off so that the stitches on display are neat and secure, and so you don't have any raw edges of your fabric showing. Below are a few examples of how you can achieve this.

If you are making a sewn item or rug, I recommend hemming or binding the edges. However, for something like the wall hanging, bunting or hung embroidery hoops, gluing the edges to the back should suffice.

TIDYING UP YOUR STITCHES

Some of the edges of your motifs may need tidying up with the needle to help distinguish them from the stitches surrounding them. To do this, gently pull away the 'border' stitches of the motif from the surrounding stitches with the tip of the punch needle and your finger.

GLUING

You shouldn't need to glue your piece as all your stitches will be secure, but if you feel it will be getting a lot of wear you might want to coat the back with a thin layer of glue. Make sure all your yarn ends are trimmed.

1 Flip the project so the side NOT on display is facing. Prepare your glue – this could be either a rug adhesive or PVA glue.

2 Spread a thin coat of glue over the stitches. Leave to dry completely.

BINDING

This kind of finish makes a feature of your edging. I often pick the yarn colour that I used for my background, but you could use a contrasting colour for a striking effect.

1 Cut around the project so you have a 3cm (1⅛in) border of fabric all around. Flip the project so the side NOT on display is facing. Fold the edges of the fabric over once by 1.5cm (about ⅝in), then again to double hem. Pin in place.

2 Thread your wool needle with your chosen yarn colour. Push your needle into the fold of the fabric and pull through; this will pull the knot into the fold of the fabric (for demonstration, mine is on show). Bring the needle up and over and into the fold, close to where you first inserted the needle. Repeat all the way around.

3 To finish the end of your yarn, whether you've come to the end of your length of threaded yarn or completed your border, take your wool needle through several stitches then cut the yarn flush.

HEMMING

Hemming the edge of the design not only prevents the fabric edges from fraying (which can easily happen with loose weave fabrics), it creates a neat, border-free finish.

 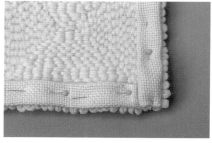 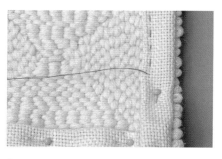

1 Cut around the project so you have a 2cm (¾in) border. Flip the project so the side NOT on display is facing. Fold one edge of the fabric over once by 1cm (⅛in), then again to double hem.

2 Pin the folded fabric in place. Repeat for the remaining edges.

3 Thread a small hand needle with some cotton thread that matches or co-ordinates with the yarn in your work. Knot the end of your thread and bring your needle up from behind the folded fabric, between the front and back of the work. Create small running stitches along the top of the folded fabric. This will hold your excess fabric in place and will leave you with a loop stitch edge.

> ## TIP
> Hemming and binding can go hand in hand if you're sewing an item where both the main and backing fabrics are loose weave. Once you've hemmed both fabrics and sewn them together, bind the edges of the turned-through project for a bound, decorative border.

Making tassels

Most of you will be familiar with making pompoms and tassels, both of which are used for some of the projects in this book. However, some of you may be unfamiliar with making tassels with the tassel-making tool below. Here is how I use it.

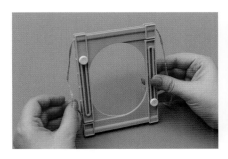

1 Place a 30cm (12in) length of your chosen yarn colour along the ridge at the top of the tassel maker.

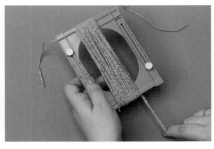

2 Directly from your ball of yarn, wind the yarn around your tassel maker as shown, as many times as you wish. The more wraps, the thicker your tassel will be.

3 Take the ends of the 30cm (12in) yarn from step 1 and tie them tightly together.

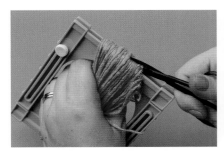

4 At the other end, cut through the wrapped yarn with a sharp pair of scissors, along the channel at the base of the tassel maker.

5 Gently remove your tassel from the tassel maker and pull the top yarn tightly once again, to ensure your tassel is secure. Take a very long length of doubled yarn and tie it around the tassel, about a third of the way down. Wrap the doubled yarn several times around the tassel.

6 Once you are happy with the number of wraps, tie the doubled yarn into a tight knot. Tuck the ends under and through the bottom of the wrapped section to secure them in place – a wool needle will help with this. Finish the tassel by trimming the bottom evenly to create a neat edge.

INSPIRATION & DESIGN

I find the process of designing and coming up with ideas is equally as fun as actually making the projects! Designing isn't as frightening as it sounds, and I hope that you play around with your yarns, yarn colours, fabrics and motifs to create your own original pieces. The projects in this book are designed to be adapted and experimented with – why not punch needle the design from the Lemon Purse (see page 56) onto a pillow instead?

inspirational items

My design influences vary – it could be the texture or shape of an item, its colour palette or use of colour, or a pattern or style on the surface.

WHERE TO FIND IT?

You can find inspiration everywhere, you just need to keep your eyes peeled and your mind open. Going for a short walk and being with nature, or wandering through town people watching or having a coffee in the local café can spark ideas when you least expect it. I try to keep a little sketchbook and pencil with me all the time for this reason – you never know when that great idea will come, and you definitely don't want to forget it!

COLOUR

I often get asked how I come up with the colour combinations for my work. Colour choice is my favourite part of designing a project – pulling out all my yarns and combining them to create the perfect palette.

Sometimes I will be inspired by the colour on something I have seen and will take a photo to remember it; or, it will just be a case of trial and error. You will notice in this book the projects are all made with a limited colour palette.

Please don't feel like you have to stick to the colours I have used. Experiment with new colour combinations and see what you come up with

my sketchbook and equipment
Use sketchbooks or design boards as a way of gathering all your ideas.

FORMING YOUR DESIGNS

Once I have an idea I often sit down with my sketches and plan how I want the final piece to look. This doesn't always happen, and if I find that I am struggling I will pull all my art materials out of the cupboard and spend the afternoon playing around.

I love to work with different mediums, especially if they are different to what the final piece will be made from. For example, I experimented a lot with collage and watercolours for the projects in this book. The process can be extremely therapeutic, and you never know when the ideas will come.

Don't throw any of your sketches or collages away; you might come back to them one day and they will spark off a whole new idea, and the process starts again.

SIMPLE PILLOW

Punching into a ready-made cover is a great project to start your punch needle journey, as there is no need for any sewing (although I have included advice on how to do this, if you do want to make your own cover). The once-neutral pillow cover looks great with these bold simple shapes, and it's so quick to make that you'll be ready to jazz up an old chair in no time.

SIZE

• 50cm (20in) square

YOU WILL NEED

• 50cm (20in) square ready-made linen pillow cover – if you'd like to make your own cover, you will need 1m (1yd) length of at least 120cm (47¼in) wide linen fabric

• Pillow inner, 50cm (20in) square

• Scissors

• Marker pen

• Embroidery hoop, 25cm (10in) in diameter

• Oxford Punch needle, #10 regular

• Wool needle

• Yarn (see details and generic alternatives on page 10):

- Rico Fashion Linen Swell Aran in 004 Salmon
- Knitcraft Everyday DK in Mint Green
- DMC Natura Just Cotton Medium in 09
- West Yorkshire Spinners Re:Treat in Mellow

DESIGN OUTLINE

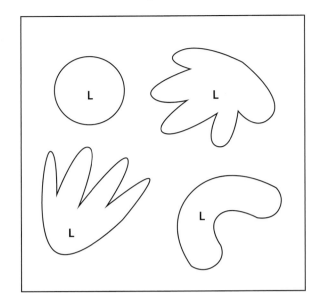

For corresponding templates, see Template Sheet B.

L = loops

COLOUR CHART

WHAT TO DO:

STEP 1
Turn your ready-made pillow cover inside out and trace your pattern onto the fabric. Unless you are using a combination of loop and embroidery stitches, remember that every motif you punch needle on the 'front' will be reversed on the 'back (the side to be on display). I chose to fill the right side of my pillow entirely with loop stitches.

STEP 2
Secure the fabric in the embroidery hoop. Make sure the fabric is nice and tight – it will slip occasionally when you start to punch needle, so you will need to tighten the hoop a couple of times.

STEP 3
Thread your punch needle with the appropriate colour then work on a shape at a time, completing the outline of the shape first then working inwards. If you are using the same yarns as I am, to have the correct thickness of yarn you might have to double the yarns for some of the shapes.

STEP 4
Once you have completed all four shapes, fasten off the yarn tails and cut them flush against the loops, as per page 22, so that they are the same height as the loops you have punched. Turn through the pillow cover so that the right side is facing out.

STEP 5
Once you are happy with your stitches, insert your pillow inner.

MAKING YOUR OWN PILLOW COVER

Cut a 60cm (23⅝in) square from the linen fabric. Frame it in the hoop, and follow the steps opposite to punch needle the main design.

Once you have completed the punch needling, cut two more pieces of linen measuring 52 x 32cm (20½ x 12⅝in). Hem both pieces along one of the longer sides by 1cm (⅜in).

Take the square of fabric with the punch-needled design then trim the fabric all around until you have a 53cm (20½in) square; this will give you a 1cm (⅜in) seam when it comes to sewing the pillow cover later. Lay the trimmed design on the table with the right side facing up. Place the two smaller pieces of linen on top, their right sides facing the punch needle design. These smaller linen pieces will overlap – this is correct, and is how you will create the envelope opening for the pillow inner. Pin the fabric edges together.

Sew all around the edges. Trim the corners diagonally, taking care to not cut through your stitches.

Turn the pillow right side out. Insert your pillow inner.

HOOP ART TRIO

These abstract pieces of art will look lovely in your living room hung individually or as a cluster of three. These are a great way to experiment with texture in your work.

SIZES

- Large hoop, 28cm (11in)
- Medium hoop, 20cm (9in)
- Small hoop, 15cm (6in)

YOU WILL NEED

- Monk's cloth, 50 x 140cm (17¾ x 55in)
- Scissors
- Marker pen
- Three embroidery hoops, 28cm (11in), 20cm (9in) and 15cm (6in) in diameter
- Adjustable punch needle – I am using the wooden adjustable punch needle
- Wool needle
- Glue gun and hot-glue, or strong craft glue
- Yarn (see details and generic alternatives on page 10):
  - *West Yorkshire Spinners Re:Treat in Mellow*
  - *Women's Institute Soft and Chunky in Cream*
  - *Knitcraft Everyday DK in Mint Green*

DESIGN OUTLINES

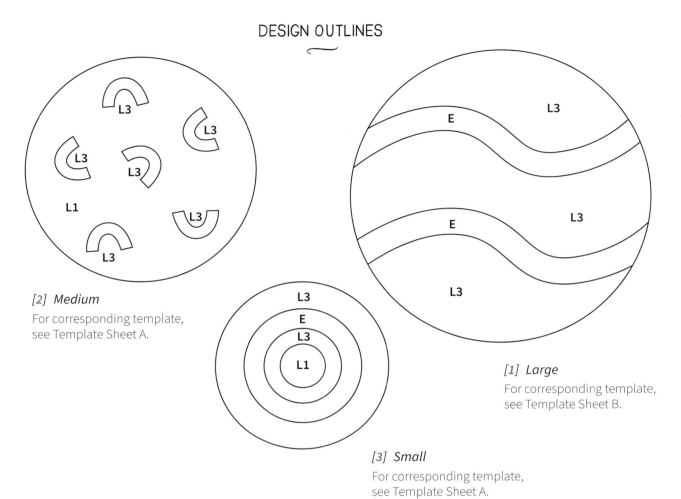

[2] Medium

For corresponding template,
see Template Sheet A.

[1] Large

For corresponding template,
see Template Sheet B.

[3] Small

For corresponding template,
see Template Sheet A.

L = loop stitches, numbers indicate loop height
(please refer to the loop-height diagram on page 24)
E = embroidery stitches

COLOUR CHARTS

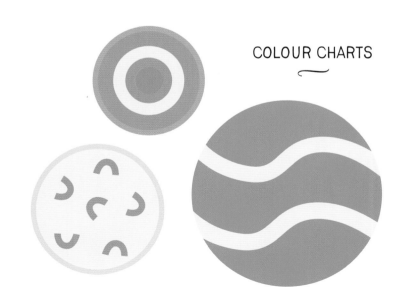

TIP

When you are using different
loop heights, you may need to
trim a few of the loops a little
to keep the heights consistent
throughout the embroidery.

WHAT TO DO:

STEP 1
Insert your monk's cloth fabric into the largest embroidery hoop. Making sure that the fabric is nice and tight, trace your design onto the fabric. Remember that every motif you punch needle on the 'front' will be reversed on the 'back' (the side to be on display), so it may be useful to write the letters of the stitches on your fabric, too, to make sure you punch on the correct side.

STEP 2
Using the adjustable punch needle, thread the gold yarn onto your needle. If the yarn is not thick enough, you will need to twist together two yarns and thread them at the same time. With the needle set on loop height 3, start to punch the 'L' sections on your fabric, using the [**1**] diagram opposite to help you. Remember to work the outlines first, then work towards the middle of the shapes.

STEP 3
Once you have finished these sections, turn your hoop over so that the yellow loops are facing you. Thread your needle with the cream yarn. This time you may need to use just the one strand of yarn. Fill in the 'E' sections, using the [**1**] diagram opposite to help you. This will create neat embroidery stitches on the 'right' side of the fabric, and make a nice contrast to the loops.

STEP 4
Once the large embroidery hoop design is fully punched, fasten off all the yarn tails and cut them flush against the loops, as per page 22. Make sure the right side of your design is on the display side of the hoop – you might need to take your fabric out of the hoop and flip it over and secure it back in the hoop. Trim so that you have a 1.5cm (⅝in) border of excess fabric all the way around. Heat up the glue gun and hot-glue, or take the strong craft glue, and adhere the border of excess fabric to the inner hoop on the wrong side of the design.

STEP 5
Using diagrams [**2**] and [**3**] and the colour charts to help you, follow the same process to create the medium and small hoops. If you wish, change the height setting on your adjustable needle to create different-sized loops. If you like, deliberately make longer loops for some of the motifs, and snip through them, to create a tufted effect – I have done this with the smaller hoop's motifs.

STEP 6
If you wish, to finish, you can bind the wooden hoops all the way around with matching or co-ordinating yarn, following the instructions on page 28. As you can see, I have done this with the small and medium hoops. I have left the large hoop unbound for a nice contrast.

PLANT POT COVERS

Have some plain plant pots lying around the house? Why not vamp them up with these bold covers – they will also keep your plants warm and cosy all winter, too! Adapt the size of the template to fit your own pot.

SIZE

- Each cover is 35 x 11cm (13¾ x 4¼in), for a 10cm (4in) diameter plant pot

YOU WILL NEED

- Monk's cloth, 50 x 140cm (17¾ x 55in) – this is enough for all three covers, but use less if you wish to make fewer
- Scissors
- Marker pen
- Large wooden frame
- Drawing pins/thumbtacks, or staples and staple gun
- Oxford Punch Needle, #10 regular
- Wool needle
- Glue gun and hot-glue, or strong craft glue
- 16cm (6¼in) length of 3mm (⅛in) wide cotton rope, per cover
- One to three buttons
- Felt, 34 x 10cm (13⅜ x 4in) per cover
- Hand-sewing needle and co-ordinating cotton thread
- Yarn (see details and generic alternatives on page 10):

  - Glitter 4ply Metallic Yarn in 8F1 Coral
  - Knitcraft Everyday DK in Mint Green
  - Women's Institute Soft and Chunky in Cream
  - DMC Natura Just Cotton Medium in 87

DESIGN OUTLINES

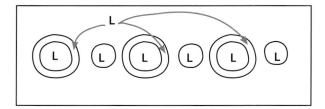

[1] Circles

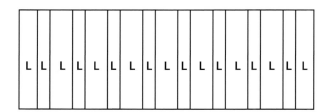

[2] Stripes

[3] Leaves

For corresponding templates, see Template Sheet B.

L = loops

COLOUR CHARTS

WHAT TO DO:

STEP 1

Stretch your monk's cloth over your wooden frame and secure it in place with drawing pins/thumbtacks or staples. Trace your chosen plant pot cover design (or all three!) onto the fabric – if you are making more than one cover, leave a 5–7.5cm (2–3in) space in between each cover. Remember that every design you punch needle on the 'front' will be reversed on the 'back' (the side to be on display).

STEP 2

Thread your punch needle with the desired colour and punch needle the small motifs first in your chosen cover. With the striped cover, punch needle all one colour first, and then fill in the gaps with the other stripe colour. Once the details are complete, punch needle the background. Remember to work all the outlines to begin with, then work your way towards the middle.

STEP 3

Once the design is fully punched, fasten off all the yarn tails and cut them flush against the loops, as per page 22. Take the punched monk's cloth off the wooden frame and trim the fabric, leaving a 2cm (¾in) border of fabric all around each cover. Hem the plant pot cover or covers, following the instructions on page 28.

STEP 4

Heat up the glue gun and hot-glue, or take the strong craft glue. Fold the 16cm (6¼in) length of rope in half and glue the ends centrally to one short end of a punched cover, on the wrong side of the fabric. The ends should sit about 1–2cm (⅜–¾in) within the cover, to attach them securely. Leave to dry.

STEP 5

Centre and glue the piece of felt to the wrong side of the punched cover. This will create a neat back for the cover and secure the hemming stitches.

STEP 6

To finish off, sew a button onto the other short end of the cover, this time on the right side of the punch-needled fabric. Make sure to wrap the cover around your pot first then mark the placement of the button where the loop of the rope sits, to ensure you sew the button in the right place.

WALL HANGING

I absolutely love a gallery wall, and I think this wall hanging would be a perfect piece to hang alongside all the other pieces of art in your home.
And you can boast that you made it too!

SIZE

- 38 x 44cm (15 x 17¼ in), excluding dowel rod

YOU WILL NEED

- Monk's cloth, 50 x 60cm (19¾ x 23¾in)
- Scissors
- Marker pen
- Large wooden frame
- Adjustable punch needle – I am using the wooden adjustable punch needle
- Wool needle
- Drawing pins/thumbtacks, or staples and staple gun
- Hand-sewing needle and matching cotton thread
- Wooden dowel, 42cm (16½in) long and 2cm (¾in) in diameter
- Yarn (see details and generic alternatives on page 10):
  - *Rico Fashion Linen Swell Aran in 004 Salmon*
  - *Women's Institute Soft and Chunky in Cream*
  - *DMC Natura Just Cotton Medium in 87*
  - *West Yorkshire Spinners Re:Treat in Mellow*

DESIGN OUTLINE

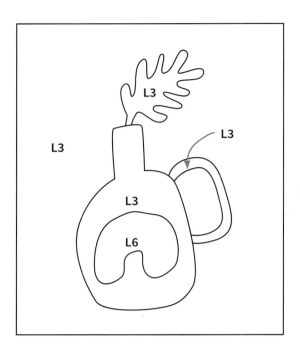

For corresponding template, see Template Sheet B.

L = loop stitches, numbers indicate loop height
(please refer to the loop-height diagram on page 24)

COLOUR CHART

TIP

To hang your wall hanging from some string, take approximately 50cm (19¾in) of twine and knot it to each end of the dowelling. It's then ready to hang!

WHAT TO DO:

STEP 1

Secure your piece of monk's cloth to your large wooden frame using drawing pins or a staple gun. Trace your design onto the fabric. Remember that every motif you punch needle on the 'front' will be reversed on the 'back' (the side to be on display).

STEP 2

With your adjustable needle set on loop height 6, start by punch needling the pink section, establishing the outline first then working your way inwards. Once this motif is complete, punch in the jug then the leaf with your adjustable needle set to loop height 3. When all the details of the wall hanging are in place, punch in the background.

STEP 3

Once you are happy with your loops, fasten off all yarn tails and cut them flush against the loops, as per page 22.

STEP 4

Take your wall hanging off the wooden frame and trim down the monk's cloth, leaving a 4cm (1½in) border of fabric all around. Hem the fabric with a sewing needle and thread that matches the background yarn colour, following the instructions on page 28.

STEP 5

With your wool needle and background yarn colour, sew the wall hanging to the wooden dowel using the binding stitch on page 28. Your wall hanging is now ready to hang – either slip the dowel over a nail, or follow the tip above.

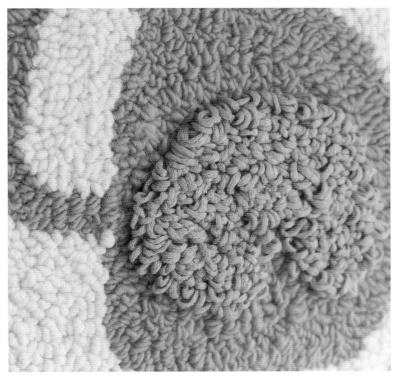

GLASSES CASE

Always losing your glasses case? Why not make this slip case for your sunglasses or reading glasses – I guarantee you will not lose this one, thanks to its bold colour scheme. It's a great project that allows you to experiment with the embroidery stitches, too.

SIZE

- 20 x 10cm (8 x 4in)

YOU WILL NEED

- Monk's cloth, 60cm (23¾in) square
- Scissors
- Marker pen
- Embroidery hoop, 25cm (10in) in diameter
- Oxford Punch Needle, #14 fine
- Wool needle
- Salmon-coloured backing fabric,
  24 x 14cm (9½ x 5½cm)
- Pale blue lining fabric, two pieces measuring
  24 x 14cm (9½ x 5½cm)
- Sewing machine
- Dressmaking pins
- Yarn (see details and generic alternatives on page 10):
  - *Rico Fashion Linen Swell Aran in 004 Salmon*
  - *Knitcraft Everyday DK in Mint Green*
  - *DMC Natura Just Cotton Medium in 87*

DESIGN OUTLINE

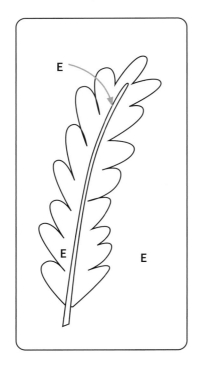

COLOUR CHART

For corresponding template, see Template Sheet B.

E = embroidery stitches

WHAT TO DO:

STEP 1

Place your monk's cloth into the embroidery hoop, stretching the fabric taut. Trace your design onto the fabric – remember, for this project, the flat stitches you punch on the 'front' of your fabric will be the side on display.

> ### TIP
>
> As this design uses the embroidery stitches for the right side, and not the loop side, you might want to use a finer pen so that the ink doesn't show through the stitches.

STEP 2

For this glasses case we are using embroidery stitches for the right side of the design. This means the side you are punching from will be on display, so try to keep the size of the stitches neat and of the same length. Thread your Oxford Punch Needle with the leaf vein colour and punch this in place. Change the yarn colour then punch needle the rest of the leaf motif, establishing the outline first then working your way inwards. Finally, fill in the background with the remaining yarn colour.

STEP 3

Once you have completed the punch needling, release the fabric from the hoop. Trim the monk's cloth, leaving a 2cm (¾in) border all the way around. If necessary, cut the lining and backing fabrics to the same size.

STEP 4

Pin the punch needled glasses case front and one lining piece together, right sides facing then sew across the top short end with your sewing machine. Repeat with the backing fabric and the second piece of lining.

STEP 5

Press these two seams flat with an iron then lay the two sections right sides together, the punched monk's cloth against the backing piece and lining against lining. Make sure the seams of the lining are identical on both pieces. Pin the pieces together.

STEP 6

Sew the two sections together all the way round, leaving a small gap at the bottom of the lining. Turn the glasses cover through the gap in the lining, so the right sides are facing out. Machine-sew the gap closed then push the lining inside the case to finish.

LION TOY

Mr Lion is such an adorable little toy that any child would love to receive him as a gift. Or why not make him for yourself – you're never too old for soft toys.
Look at that little face!

SIZE

- 19 x 18cm (7½ x 7in)

YOU WILL NEED

- Monk's cloth, 50cm (19¾in) square
- Scissors
- Marker pen
- Embroidery hoop, 25cm (10in) in diameter
- Oxford Punch Needle, #10 regular
- Wool needle
- Dressmaking pins
- Yellow backing fabric, 24 x 22cm (9½ x 8¾cm)
- Patterned fabric for the bow tie, 10 x 20cm (4 x 8in)
- Sewing machine
- Hand-sewing needle and matching cotton thread
- 20cm (8in) length of 12mm (½in) rope
- Toy stuffing
- Yarn (see details and generic alternatives on page 10):
  - *West Yorkshire Spinners Re:Treat in Mellow*
  - *Women's Institute Soft and Chunky in Cream*
  - *Lily Sugar 'n Cream in Jute*
  - *Anchor Creativa Fino 4ply in Fawn*

DESIGN OUTLINE

PL

E

E

E

L

COLOUR CHART

For corresponding template, see Template Sheet A.

PL = pulled loop stitches
L = loop stitches
E = embroidery stitches

TIP

With projects that require a combination of embroidery and loop stitches, it is helpful to trace the pattern onto both sides of the monk's cloth. You can use this to your advantage later, when sewing the punch-needled fabric to the backing fabric, as you will see the outline of the lion clearly.

WHAT TO DO:

STEP 1
Stretch your fabric into your embroidery hoop, making sure it's nice and tight. Trace your pattern onto the fabric. Remember that the lion's face is made with embroidery stitches, and will be worked first; so, you will need to remove the fabric and hoop it once again to work the rest of the body, which is made with loop stitches.

STEP 2
Thread your Oxford Punch Needle with cream yarn then punch needle the whole face of the lion, using embroidery stitches to create a flat surface. Using the wool needle and some brown yarn, stitch the eyes, nose and mouth lines over the embroidery stitches.

STEP 3
Remove the fabric from the hoop, flip it over and re-hoop it. Punch needle around the face and body with the taupe yarn; this will create fluffy loops for the body.

STEP 4
To create the mane, thread the punch needle with gold yarn and punch through the fabric. Leave the needle in the fabric. With the other hand, pinch the loop and pull it to create a very long loop. Carefully lift the punch needle, holding the long loop as you move towards the next stitch. Repeat this technique, working your way around the face, to create the large yellow mane.

STEP 5
Once you are happy with your punch needled lion, fasten off the yarn ends and trim them flush against the loops, as per page 22. Release your fabric from the embroidery hoop.

STEP 6
Pin the lion to the backing fabric, right sides together. Sewing close to the loop stitches, sew around the lion with a sewing machine to join him to the backing fabric, leaving a 10cm (4in) gap in one straight edge. Be careful not to catch the mane as you sew. Once finished, trim the backing fabric all around to the shape of the lion, adding a 1cm (⅜in) seam allowance.

STEP 7
Turn the lion the right way out through the gap and stuff him with toy stuffing. Sew the gap closed with a hand-sewing needle and matching thread.

STEP 8
To make your lion a little bow tie, begin by cutting a 16 x 8cm (6¼ x 3⅛in) rectangle from the patterned fabric. Fold the fabric in half widthways, right sides together, then sew up the top and bottom edges. Turn the sewn square through the remaining open side, then machine-sew the opening closed. Roll the seam towards the middle.

STEP 9
From the remaining fabric, cut a 4 x 6cm (1½ x 2¼in) rectangle. Fold each long edge to the middle and press with an iron, then fold the piece in half lengthways and press again, to hide the folded edges in the middle.

STEP 10
Pinch the middle of the larger sewn square, then take the folded strip of fabric and wrap this around the pinched middle. Secure the two together with hand stitches. Sew the bow tie to the front of the lion with a hand-sewing needle and matching cotton thread.

STEP 11
Tie a knot at the end of the length of rope. Secure the other end to the back of the lion with overstitches, using the gold yarn and a wool needle.

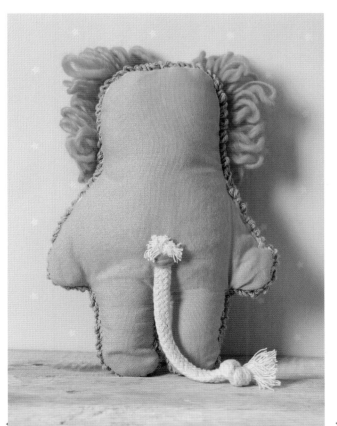

LEMON PURSE

Jazz up any outfit with this lemon slice purse. It's ideal for summer days and sunny holidays, and could even make a perfect accessory for a summer wedding. It will definitely catch people's eyes!

SIZE

- 28 x 15cm (11 x 6in)

YOU WILL NEED

- Monk's cloth, 50 x 140cm (17¾ x 55in)
- Scissors
- Marker pen
- Oxford Punch Needle, #10 regular
- Wool needle
- Embroidery hoop, 25cm (10in) in diameter
- Yellow backing fabric, 32 x 40cm (12¾ x 15¾in)
- Peach patterned lining fabric, two pieces measuring 32 x 40cm (12¾ x 15¾in)
- Dressmaking pins
- Magnetic snap clasp and pliers
- Pompom maker, 60mm/medium size
- Tassel maker, or a card or book to wrap yarn around
- Sewing machine
- Hand-sewing needle and matching cotton thread
- Yarn (see details and generic alternatives on page 10):

  - DMC Natura Just Cotton Medium in 09
  - West Yorkshire Spinners Re:Treat in Mellow
  - Women's Institute Soft and Chunky in Cream
  - Rico Fashion Linen Swell Aran in 004 Salmon

DESIGN OUTLINE

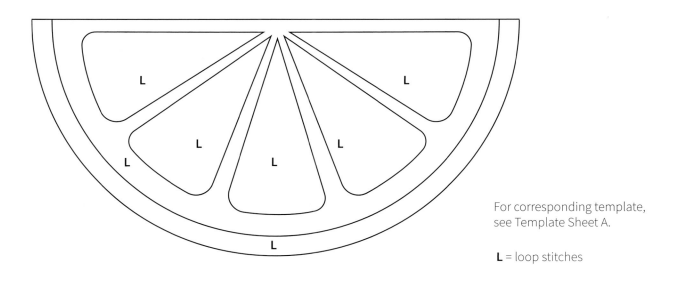

For corresponding template,
see Template Sheet A.

L = loop stitches

COLOUR CHART

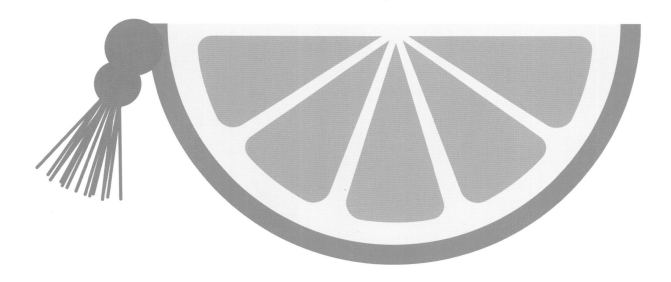

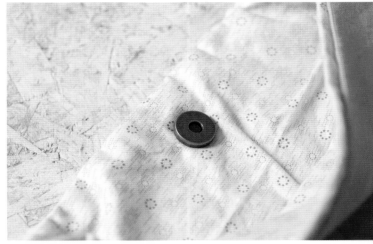

WHAT TO DO:

STEP 1
Place your monk's cloth into your large embroidery hoop. Trace your lemon design onto the fabric. Remember that every motif you punch needle on the 'front' will be reversed on the 'back' (the side to be on display). The best thing about this design is that it is symmetrical, so no worries about which way you transfer it!

STEP 2
Thread your Oxford Punch Needle with the yellow yarn then punch needle the yellow lemon segments. Once they are complete, punch needle the cream 'pith' around them. Finish off the lemon by punch needling the mustard 'outer skin'. Once the design is complete, fasten off all the yarn tails and trim them flush against the loops, as per page 22.

STEP 3
Release the fabric from the embroidery hoop and trim the fabric, leaving a 2cm (¾in) border of fabric all around. Cut the piece of backing fabric and the two pieces of lining fabric to the same shape and size as the trimmed monk's cloth.

STEP 4
Place the lemon and one lining piece right sides together and pin along the straight top edge. Sew them together using a sewing machine, sewing close to the loop stitches. Repeat this with the backing fabric and the other piece of lining.

STEP 5
Attach one side of your magnetic snap clasp to the top of each lining piece, about 4cm (1½in) down from the seam and centred: place the metal support of one snap half onto the wrong side of one lining piece and mark its spot through the 'slits' either side of the central circle. Snip the slits with scissors. Insert the prongs of the snap into the slits from the right side of the fabric. Push the metal support over the prongs on the wrong side of the fabric,

then bend the prongs inwards or outwards with pliers to secure the snap. Repeat on the other piece of lining with the remaining half of the snap clasp, ensuring the pieces line up.

STEP 6
Press these two seams flat with an iron then lay the two sections right sides together, the punched lemon against the backing piece and lining against lining. Make sure the seams of the lining are identical on both pieces. Pin the pieces together.

STEP 7
Pin the two pieces of fabric right sides together then sew all around the perimeter of the two sections, leaving a 10cm (4in) gap in the bottom of the lining. Turn the purse the right way out through the gap, then hand- or machine-sew the opening closed.

STEP 8
To finish off the purse, add a tassel and pompom decoration. To make the tassel, either you can follow the instructions on page 29 or use this traditional method: wind your chosen yarn around a book or a piece of cardboard. Tie a length of yarn around the middle of the wrapped yarn on one side, then slide it to the top. Trim through the wrapped yarn along the bottom edge of the card or book. Remove the tied yarn from the book or cardboard, then tie another length of yarn around the tassel, a third of the way down from the top. Trim the ends of the tassel to neaten.
To make a pompom, wrap your yarn around the arms of a pompom maker. Tie them together with matching yarn and trim the wrapped edges to release the pompom.
Thread the hanging end of the tassel onto a wool needle and take it through the pompom and knot off. Sew the joined tassel and pompom to the corner of the bag with a hand-sewing needle and matching thread.

SHELL PILLOW

Living by the beach, I find it extremely hard to not pick up shells that catch my eye. Bring the seaside into your home with this brightly coloured, shell-shaped pillow. I have added some metallic yarn, to mimic the pearlescent details you find on real shells.

SIZE

- 36 x 40cm (14¼ x 15¾in)

YOU WILL NEED

- Monk's cloth, 60 x 70cm (23¾ x 27½in)
- Scissors
- Marker pen
- Large wooden frame
- Adjustable punch needle – I am using the wooden adjustable punch needle
- Wool needle
- Drawing pins/thumbtacks, or staples and staple gun
- Peach-coloured backing fabric, 40 x 44cm (15¾ x 17½in)
- Dressmaking pins
- Stuffing
- Sewing machine
- Hand-sewing needle and matching cotton thread
- Yarn (see details and generic alternatives on page 10):
  - *Rico Fashion Linen Swell Aran in 004 Salmon*
  - *Glitter 4ply Metallic Yarn in 8F1 Coral*
  - *Wendy Purity in 5165 Breeze*

DESIGN OUTLINE

COLOUR CHART

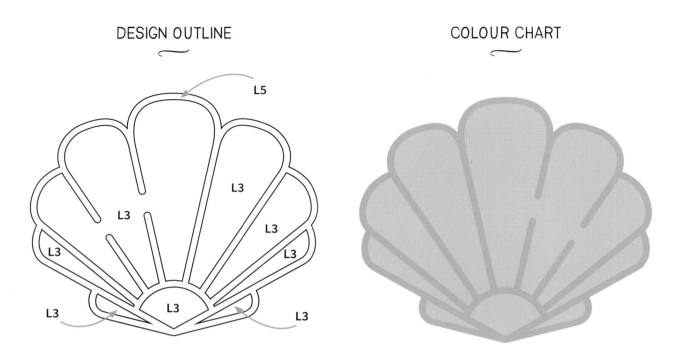

For corresponding template, see Template Sheet A.

L = loop stitches, numbers indicate loop height
(please refer to the loop-height diagram on page 24)

WHAT TO DO:

STEP 1
Stretch the monk's cloth over your wooden frame and secure in place with drawing pins/thumbtacks or staples. Make sure the fabric is nice and tight. If it starts to become baggy you can easily re-tighten as you work. Once the fabric is taut, trace the shell design onto the cloth – remember that every motif you punch needle on the 'front' will be reversed on the 'back' (the side to be on display).

STEP 2
Thread the adjustable punch needle with doubled dark pink yarn. Set the loop height to 5 then punch needle the outline of the shell. The loops will be nice and long on the other side.

STEP 3
Once you have completed the outline, thread your needle with two different yarns – the lighter pink yarn and the metallic pink yarn. Set the loop height to 3, then punch needle the rest of the pillow. Remember to work the outlines of the motifs first, then work your way towards the middle.

STEP 4
When the design is complete, fasten off all the yarn tails and trim them to the height of the loops, as per page 22.

STEP 5
Take the monk's cloth off the wooden frame and trim down the fabric, leaving a 2cm (¾in) border all the way around.

STEP 6
Cut the backing fabric to the same shape and size as the punched monk's cloth. Pin the backing fabric to the shell with the fabrics right sides together. Sew all the way around the shell, leaving a 10cm (4in) gap in one straighter side. Turn the shell the right side out through the gap.

STEP 7
Stuff the pillow with toy stuffing until it's nice and plump, then hand-sew the gap closed using a hand-sewing needle and matching thread – squeeze in more stuffing before completely sewing up the pillow, if you wish, to make the pillow nice and plump. Trim any loose or larger loops to finish, so they are all consistent and neat.

PUNCHED JACKET PATCH

I really like to upcycle clothes, and this project is a perfect way to jazz up any old piece of clothing that you have lying around. I love how the patch looks on this denim jacket, and would be proud to wear it any day.

SIZE

- 28 x 38cm (11 x 15¾in), including fringing

YOU WILL NEED

- Monk's cloth, 50 x 140cm (17¾ x 55in)
- Scissors
- Marker pen
- Large wooden frame
- Adjustable punch needle – I am using the wooden adjustable punch needle
- Drawing pins/thumbtacks, or staples and staple gun
- Wool needle
- Dressmaking pins
- Hand-sewing needle and matching cotton thread
- Yarn (see details and generic alternatives on page 10):
  - *Knitcraft Everyday DK in Mint Green*
  - *West Yorkshire Spinners Re:Treat Yarn in Mellow*
  - *Women's Institute Soft and Chunky in Cream*
  - *Rico Fashion Linen Swell Aran in 004 Salmon*

DESIGN OUTLINE

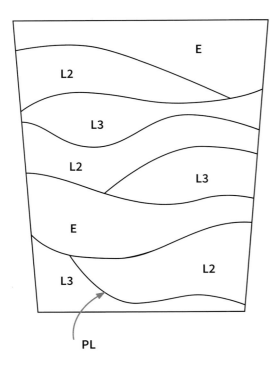

E

L2

L3

L2

L3

E

L2

L3

PL

COLOUR CHART

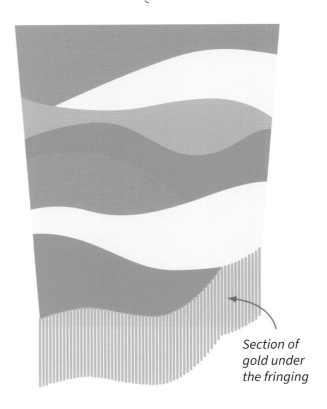

Section of gold under the fringing

For the corresponding template, see Template Sheet B.

PL = pulled loop stitches
L = loop stitches, numbers indicate loop height
(please refer to the loop-height diagram on page 24)
E = embroidery stitches

TIP

If you're nervous about making extra large loops, you could create lots of thin tassels and sew these to the bottom of your patch instead. Or, for an even jazzier effect, pompoms!

WHAT TO DO:

STEP 1

Stretch your monk's cloth over a large wooden frame, making sure that your fabric is nice and tight. Secure the fabric in place with drawing pins/thumbtacks or staples. Trace the design onto the fabric – remember you will be using both sides of the monk's cloth so you might need to trace it onto both sides.

Note also that you may need to tweak the size of the design to fit the back section of your jacket, too.

STEP 2

Working from the top of the design to the bottom with your adjustable punch needle, fill in the shapes on your transferred design with the necessary yarn colour. Remember to establish the outlines first then work your way towards the middle. Alternate between loop and embroidery stitches with each shape to create texture, and make sure to flip the fabric over to form the embroidery stitches on the correct side of the fabric. Adjust the loop heights, too, so you can create even more height in your work.

STEP 3

When you reach the border between the penultimate salmon section and the final bottom gold section, punch through the fabric with the gold colour and leave your needle there. With your other hand, hold onto the loop of yarn under the fabric and pull it to create a very long loop. Continue to punch two rows in this way to create the fringing on your patch. Once these rows are complete, continue to punch the rest of the final section with the gold yarn, following the regular technique.

STEP 4

When the design is complete, fasten off all the yarn tails and trim them to the height of the loops, as per page 22.

STEP 5

Take the punched cloth off the wooden frame and trim the fabric, leaving a 2cm (¾in) border of fabric all around. Hem the edges of the patch with a hand-sewing needle and matching thread, as per page 28.

STEP 6

Pin the hemmed patch to the back of your jacket. With the hand-sewing needle and thread, attach the patch to the back of your jacket by sewing around the edges with close overstitches.

RUG

I love this Matisse-inspired rug, and it would look great in any room. This would also look fantastic as a wall hanging if you don't like the idea of people walking all over your hard work!

SIZE

- 60 x 44cm (23½ x 17¼in), not including tassels

YOU WILL NEED

- Monk's cloth, 1 x 1.4m (1 x 1½yd)
- Scissors
- Marker pen
- Oxford Punch Needle, #10 regular
- Wool needle
- Large wooden frame
- Drawing pins/thumbtacks, or staples and staple gun
- Tassel maker, or a card or book to wrap yarn around
- Hand-sewing needle and matching cotton thread
- Yarn (see details and generic alternatives on page 10):

    - Knitcraft Everyday DK in Mint Green
    - West Yorkshire Spinners Re:Treat Yarn in Mellow
    - DMC Natura Just Cotton Medium in 09
    - Women's Institute Soft and Chunky in Cream
    - Wendy Purity in 5165 Breeze
    - Rico Fashion Linen Swell Aran in 004 Salmon

DESIGN OUTLINE

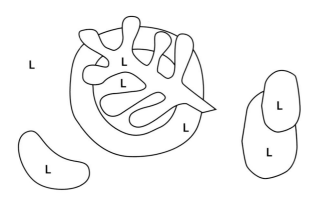

COLOUR CHART

For corresponding template,
see Template Sheet A.
Please note, only the motifs – not the
outline of the rug – are included on
the sheet.

L = loop stitches

WHAT TO DO:

STEP 1

Stretch your monk's cloth across the wooden frame, ensuring the fabric is nice and tight. Secure in place with drawing pins/thumbtacks or staples. Remember you can always adjust the drawing pins/thumbtacks or re-staple if you feel the fabric is not tight enough. Trace the rug design onto the monk's cloth. Remember that every motif you punch needle on the 'front' will be reversed on the 'back' (the side to be on display).

STEP 2

Thread the Oxford Punch Needle with the necessary yarn colour then punch in all the small motifs to begin with. Remember to establish the outlines first then work your way towards the middle to fill in the shapes. Once you have completed the smaller motifs, fill in the background with loop stitches until you have the desired size (if you would like to make a rug the same size as mine, please refer to the size details on page 68).

STEP 3

Fasten off all yarn tails and cut them flush against the loops, as per page 22. You might need to trim some of the loops so they are all consistent in height.

STEP 4

Take the punched rug off the frame and trim the fabric, leaving a 2cm (¾in) border of fabric all around. Bind all the edges with the same yarn used for the background colour, following the instructions on page 28.

STEP 5

Once you have finished binding all four sides, you will need to make some tassels.

Either you can follow the instructions on page 29, or use this traditional method: wind your chosen colour of yarn around a book or a piece of cardboard. Tie a length of yarn around the middle of the wrapped yarn on one side, then slide it to the top. Trim through the wrapped yarn along the bottom edge of the card or book. Remove the tied yarn from the book or cardboard, then tie another length of yarn around the tassel, a third of the way down from the top. Trim the ends of the tassel to neaten. Repeat three more times to make four tassels.

Finish the rug by sewing the hanging ends of the tassels to each corner of the rug with the wool needle.

RAINBOW DAY BAG

This small tote is the perfect accessory for any season, rain or shine! You will definitely make a statement with this project. Change the length of the leather strap if you like, making it longer for an over-the-shoulder bag, or keep it short for something that will nicely slip over your arm.

SIZE

- 33cm (13in) square, not including the strap

YOU WILL NEED

- Monk's cloth, 50 x 140cm (17¾ x 55in)
- Scissors
- Marker pen
- Large wooden frame
- Oxford Punch Needle, #10 regular
- Drawing pins/thumbtacks, or staples and staple gun
- Wool needle
- Peach-coloured backing fabric, 37cm (14¾in) square
- Pale blue lining fabric, two pieces measuring 37cm (14¾in) square
- Dressmaking pins
- Magnetic snap clasp and pliers
- Sewing machine
- Leather or faux-leather strap, 62cm (24½in) long and 2cm (¾in) wide
- Awl or leather-punch pliers
- Hand-sewing needle and co-ordinating cotton thread
- Yarn (see details and generic alternatives on page 10):
  - *Knitcraft Everyday DK in Mint Green*
  - *West Yorkshire Spinners Re:Treat in Mellow*
  - *DMC Natura Just Cotton Medium in 09*
  - *Women's Institute Soft and Chunky in Cream*
  - *Wendy Purity in 5165 Breeze*

DESIGN OUTLINE

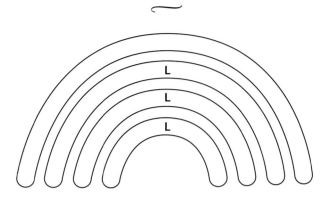

For the corresponding template, see Template Sheet A.
Please note, only the motif – not the outline of the bag –
is included on the sheet.

L = loop stitches

COLOUR CHART

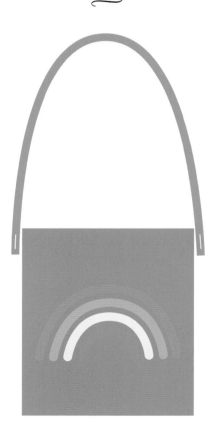

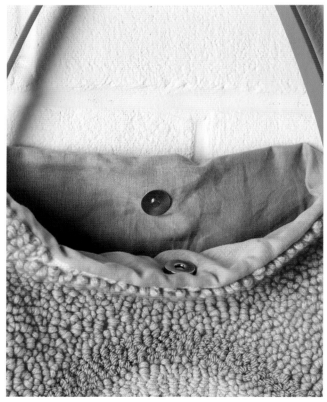

WHAT TO DO:

STEP 1
Stretch your monk's cloth over the wooden frame, ensuring the fabric is nice and tight. Secure in place with drawing pins/thumbtacks or staples. Remember you can always adjust the drawing pins/thumbtacks or re-staple the fabric if you feel it is not tight enough.

STEP 2
Trace the rainbow design onto the monk's cloth. Remember that every motif you punch needle on the 'front' will be reversed on the 'back' (the side to be on display). The best thing about this design is that it is symmetrical, so no worries about which way you transfer it!

STEP 3
Punch needle the rainbow motif to begin, establishing the outlines first before filling in the shapes. Once the stripes of the rainbow are punched, fill in the background with loop stitches until you have the desired size (if you would like to make a bag the same size as mine, please refer to the size details on page 72).

STEP 4
Once the design is complete, fasten off all yarn tails as per page 22, and trim them to the same height as the loops. You might need to trim some of the loops so they are all consistent in height.

STEP 5
Release the monk's cloth from the frame and trim down the fabric, leaving a 2cm (¾in) border all the way around. Cut one piece of backing fabric and two pieces of lining fabric to the same size as the trimmed monk's cloth.

STEP 6
Pin one piece of lining to the top of the punch needle piece, right sides together. Sew along the top, close to the loops, using your sewing machine. Repeat with the other piece of lining and the backing fabric.

STEP 7
Attach one side of your magnetic snap clasp to the top of each lining piece about 4cm (1½in) down from the seam and centred: place the metal support of one snap half onto the wrong side of one lining piece and mark its spot through the 'slits' either side of the central circle. Snip the slits with scissors. Insert the prongs of the snap into the slits from the right side of the fabric. Push the metal support over the prongs on the wrong side of the fabric, then bend the prongs inwards or outwards with pliers to secure the snap. Repeat on the other piece of lining with the remaining half of the snap clasp, ensuring the pieces line up.

STEP 8
Iron these two seams flat then pin them right sides together, the punched fabric against the backing piece and lining against lining. Make sure the seams of the lining are identical on both pieces.

STEP 9
Sew all around the perimeter of the two sections, leaving a 10cm (4in) gap in the bottom of the lining. Turn the bag the right way out through the gap then machine sew the opening closed. Push the lining inside the bag.

STEP 10
Punch two holes at each end of the leather or faux-leather strap with an awl or leather-punch pliers – one hole 2cm (¾in) up from the end, the next 6cm (2¼in) up. Approximately 8cm (3⅛in) down from the top of the bag, over each side seam, hand-sew the ends in place through the holes with co-ordinating thread. Make sure to start your sewing from the inside of the bag, taking the needle through the lining, so that the knot is not on show.

MOON BUNTING

Learn the phases of the moon with the help of this cute home accessory –
perfect for any lunar lover.

SIZE

- 1.75m (2yd) long, with each 'moon' measuring 12cm (4¾in)
in diameter

YOU WILL NEED

- Monk's cloth, 50 x 140cm (17¾ x 55in)
- Scissors
- Marker pen
- Large wooden frame
- Oxford Punch Needle, #10 regular
- Wool needle
- Drawing pins/thumbtacks, or staples and staple gun
- White felt, 36cm (14¼in) square
- Pompom maker, 45mm/small size
- Cream woven tape, 2m (2¼yd) long and 2cm (¾in) wide
- Glue gun and hot-glue, or strong craft glue
- 16 wooden beads, 2cm (¾in) in diameter
- Hand-sewing needle and co-ordinating cotton thread
- Yarn (see details and generic alternatives on page 10):
  - *Knitcraft Everyday DK in Mint Green*
  - *Women's Institute Soft and Chunky in Cream*
  - *Women's Institute Home Cotton Aran in Pewter*

DESIGN OUTLINE

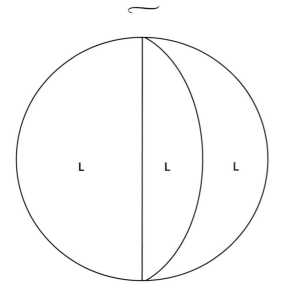

For corresponding template, see Template Sheet A.

Note that the template includes both new and full moons, and the gibbous, quarter and crescent phases. To create some of the phases, you will need to flip the template over before transferring the motif.

L = loop stitches

COLOUR CHART

New moon · **Waxing crescent** · **First quarter, or half moon** · **Waxing gibbous** · **Full moon** · **Waning gibbous** · **Third quarter, or half moon** · **Waning crescent** · **New moon**

WHAT TO DO:

STEP 1

Stretch your monk's cloth over the wooden frame, ensuring the fabric is nice and tight. Secure in place with drawing pins/thumbtacks or staples. Remember you can always adjust the drawing pins/thumbtacks or re-staple the fabric if you feel it is not tight enough.

STEP 2

Transfer the necessary moon phase onto the monk's cloth. There are nine moons to transfer overall. There will be three moons in a single colour – two new moons and one full moon – then two each of the other moon phases. For the gibbous and crescent phases, you will need to flip the templates depending on whether they are showing a waxing or waning moon. Remember that you will be punching the moon from the 'front' to create the loop stitches on the 'back', so you will need to make sure you have flipped the template correctly.

STEP 3

Punch needle all nine moons, following the colour chart above. Begin with the outline of each shape in that particular moon design before working your way inwards to fill them in. When all the moons are punch needled, fasten off all tails then cut them flush against the loops, as per page 22.

STEP 4

Take the moons off the frame then trim the fabric around each one, leaving a 2cm (¾in) border of fabric all around. Snip into the fabric every 2cm (¾in) around the moon; this will help to create a smooth circle when turning the fabric over to the wrong side.

STEP 5

Finish off all your moons by hemming the edges in a similar way to the method on page 28, this time securing each edge with a glue gun and hot-glue or strong craft glue. Use the circle template to cut out nine pieces of felt, slightly smaller than the moons, then stick them to the back of each punched moon with glue. Leave them to dry.

STEP 6

Lay out your woven tape and place your moons onto it, making sure they are evenly spaced. Using a hand-sewing needle and co-ordinating thread, sew your moons onto the woven tape.

STEP 7

Using the grey yarn and pompom maker, make eight small pompoms. Trim each one so you have perfectly round pompoms. Place a pompom between each moon then add a wooden bead to each side of it. Secure the pompoms and beads onto the woven tape using the hand-sewing needle and co-ordinating cotton thread.

STEP 8

To be able to hang your bunting you will need to create some loops at each end of your woven tape. To do this, fold the ends over by 6–8cm (2¼–3⅛in) or so, then stitch a little cross through the layers with a wool needle and matching yarn.

DEDICATION

For Alma.

I hope I can give you the creative upbringing that I have lovingly enjoyed and treasured.

ACKNOWLEDGEMENTS

Thank you to Laurie, for encouraging me, for pushing me when I needed it and for being our rock.

Also, thank you to Hobbycraft for supplying the yarn for all the projects.

First published in 2021

Search Press Limited
Wellwood, North Farm Road,
Tunbridge Wells, Kent TN2 3DR

Photographs on pages 4–39 by Mark Davison.
All remaining photographs are by Stacy Grant.
Project diagrams, colour charts and templates
© Lucy Davidson, 2021
Photographs, illustrations and design copyright
© Search Press Ltd 2021

Text copyright © Lucy Davidson, 2021

ISBN: 978-1-78221-864-7

The Publisher and author can accept no responsibility for any consequences arising from the information, advice or instructions given in this publication.

Readers are permitted to reproduce any of the items/patterns in this book for their personal use, or for the purposes of selling for charity, free of charge and without the prior permission of the Publisher. Any use of the items/patterns for commercial purposes is not permitted without the prior permission of the Publisher.

Suppliers/resources

All yarn kindly gifted from Hobbycraft –
  www.hobbycraft.co.uk
(Apart from the glitter metallic cone, this is from Airedale Wools) –
  www.airedalewools.co.uk
Monk's cloth –
  www.wholepunching.co.uk
  www.ragrugsuk.co.uk
For details of alternative suppliers, please visit the
Search Press website:
  www.searchpress.com

Metric/imperial conversions

The projects in this book have been made using metric measurements, and the imperial equivalents provided have been calculated following standard conversion practices. The imperial measurements are often rounded to the nearest $\frac{1}{8}$in for ease of use except in the rare circumstance; however, if you need more exact measurements, there are a number of excellent online converters that you can use. Always use either metric or imperial, not a combination of both.

Find out more about Lucy and her work
Website – www.peasandneedles.co.uk
Pinterest – www.pinterest.co.uk/peasandneedles
Facebook – @peasandneedleblog
Twitter – @peasandneedles
Instagram –@peasandneedles